A Note to Parents

Dorling Kindersley Readers is a compelling new program for beginning readers, designed in conjunction with leading literacy experts, including Dr. Linda Gambrell, President of the National Reading Conference and past board member of the International Reading Association.

Beautiful illustrations and superb full-color photographs combine with engaging, easy-to-read stories to offer a fresh approach to each subject in the series. Each *Dorling Kindersley Reader* is guaranteed to capture a child's interest while developing his or her reading skills, general knowledge, and love of reading.

The four levels of *Dorling Kindersley Readers* are aimed at different reading abilities, enabling you to choose the books that are exactly right for your child:

Level 1 for **Preschool to Grade 1**
Level 2 for **Grades 1 to 3**
Level 3 for **Grades 2 and 3**
Level 4 for **Grades 2 to 4**

The "normal" age at which a child begins to read can be anywhere from three to eight years old, so these levels are intended only as a general guideline.

No matter which level you select, you can be sure that you are helping your child learn to read, then read to learn!

A DORLING KINDERSLEY BOOK
www.dk.com

Project Editor Louise Pritchard
Art Editor Jill Plank

Senior Editor Linda Esposito
Senior Art Editor
Diane Thistlethwaite
US Editor Regina Kahney
Production Melanie Dowland
Picture Researcher Liz Moore
Illustrator Peter Dennis
Indexer Lynn Bresler

Reading Consultant
Linda B. Gambrell, Ph.D.

First American Edition, 2000
2 4 6 8 10 9 7 5 3 1
Published in the United States by Dorling Kindersley Publishing, Inc.
95 Madison Avenue, New York, New York 10016

Published in Great Britain by Dorling Kindersley Limited.

Library of Congress Cataloging-in-Publication Data
Hayden, Kate.
 Twisters! / by Kate Hayden.– 1st American ed.
 p. cm. – (Dorling Kindersley readers)
 Summary: Describes how tornadoes form and what effects they have on
people and their surroundings.
 ISBN 0-7894-5708-3 – ISBN 0-7894-5709-1 (pbk.)
 1. Tornadoes–Juvenile literature. [1. Tornadoes.] I. Title. II. Series.

QC955.2.H39 2000
551.55'3–dc21   99-086951

Color reproduction by Colourscan, Singapore
Printed and bound in China by L.Rex

The publisher would like to thank the following
for their kind permission to reproduce their photographs:
c=center; b=bottom; l=left; r=right; t=top

National Geographic Image Collection: Chris Johns 26–27b; NOAA
Photo Library/NOAA Central Library (www/photolib.noaa.gov/):
28t, 30; Planet Earth Pictures: Alex Benwell 15br, Paolo Fanciulli 7br;
Robert Harding Picture Library: 16, Sheila Beougher 18bl,
Warren Faidley/Agliolo 1br, Warren Faidley/Int'l Stock 16–17, 18tr, Jeff
Greenberg 22tr; Tony Stone Images: 21tr, Christoph Burki 5tr, Jerry
Kobalenko 4–5, John Lund 32, Alan R Moller 19b, Camille Tokerud 15cr;
Topham Picturepoint: 25br, J. McTyre 24.

DK DORLING KINDERSLEY *READERS*

BEGINNING
TO READ ALONE
2

Twisters!

Written by Kate Hayden

DK

DORLING KINDERSLEY PUBLISHING, INC.

www.dk.com

Rob was working
in his farmyard in Texas.
It was a peaceful spring day.
But his dog, Barney, was unhappy.
He hid under a tractor
and would not come out.
Rob wondered if Barney was ill.

Second sense

Animals have sharper senses than we have. Many can sense changes in the weather, like just before a bad storm.

Suddenly the sky went dark.

Hailstones as big as golf balls

pelted down from the sky.

Thunder rolled

and lightning flashed.

Then came a deathly stillness

in the air.

Somehow, Barney had known!

A moment later,
huge black clouds began to spin.
They bubbled at the top
like boiling milk.
Gusts of wind blew straw around.
Just then, a finger of cloud
spiraled down from the sky.
A twister!

Rob stood rooted to the spot.
The twister touched the ground.
Mud and grass swirled up
like smoke from a bonfire.
That was only the start.
The twister began to move.
It skipped and bounced
across the fields.
It grew bigger, faster, and dirtier
as it picked up mud
from the ground.

Waterspouts
Twisters out at sea
are called waterspouts.
They whisk up water.
The tallest one ever
seen was 1 mile high.

Rob watched in horror
as the twister went
toward his neighbor's farm.
It picked up straw, trees –
and even a farm truck.
It spun them around in its funnel.

Rob sighed with relief when
the twister moved away.
He thought he was safe.
But then the twister
changed direction –
right toward him!

Suddenly the twister was hanging

right over Rob's farm.

There was a noise

like a rushing waterfall,

then – BANG!

The barn exploded

as if a bomb had gone off inside it.

Rob ran with Barney
to the cellar in his house.
His ears were hurting
and he could hardly breathe.
That's because the air pressure
inside a twister is very low.
This makes people's ears ache
and causes buildings to explode.

 Just as Rob reached
the cellar,
his front porch flew off
with an ear-splitting CRASH!
Then came a SMASH
as the house windows blew in.
Two minutes later, all was silent.

Rob came up from the cellar.
Furniture lay smashed on the floor.
Most of the doors
and windows were gone.
Rob felt lucky
to be alive.

Neighbors helped Rob clean up.
The twister did not damage
the neighbors' house.

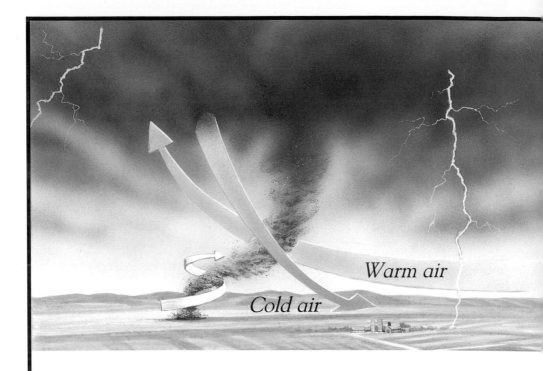

Warm air

Cold air

Twisters can form
when cold air meets warm air.
The warm air is sucked up
in a swirling column
called a funnel cloud.
It spins at great speed.
Twisters contain
the most deadly winds
in the world.

No one knows
what a twister will do next.
It can lift up a large truck
and smash it to pieces,
but leave small objects undamaged.

A twister once picked up a baby
and set him down safely
300 feet away.
The baby did not
even wake up!

Strange showers

When twisters drop
things they've picked up,
strange things can happen.
A twister in England
caused a shower of frogs.

There are lots of
strange stories
about twisters.
A twister once
blew away
a man's
birth certificate.
The twister carried it
50 miles
then dropped it
in a friend's garden.
Another twister
sucked up some roses and water
from a vase.
It dropped them in another room.
But it left the vase on the table.

One twister picked up
a jar of pickles
and carried the jar for miles
without damaging it.

Twisters come in
many different
shapes and sizes.
They can be thin,
white, and wispy.
Or they can be
big, thick,
and black.

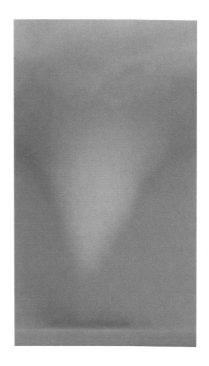

They can even
be in color!
If a twister
travels across
a muddy field,
the mud
turns it brown –
and very smelly!

Twisters can grow bigger and faster
as they go along.
Some look like they have
a loop or knot in the middle.
Some are wider at the bottom
than at the top.
Some are shaped like a tube.
Others look like a slice of pie.

Lots of people
have seen a twister
from the outside.
But only a few have looked
inside a twister and survived.

A farmer named Will Keller
once looked up into a twister
from his underground shelter.
Just as he closed
the door of his shelter,
he saw lots of mini twisters
inside the big twister.
These mini twisters can rip
through a building
and slice it to shreds.

Twister speeds

Some twisters travel
only as fast as
a person walking.
Others travel
as fast as express trains.

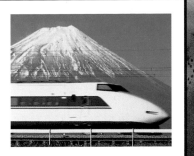

21

Home sweet home

People stay in Tornado Alley because it is their home. If their houses are destroyed, they just rebuild.

Twisters are also known as tornados. There is an area in the U.S. that is called Tornado Alley. It is famous for its deadly twisters. Up to 300 occur there every year between April and July. They kill more than 80 people.

Twisters form during these months
as warm air from the south meets
cold air from the north –
right over Tornado Alley.

TORNADO ALLEY

NEBRASKA

IOWA

KANSAS

MISSOURI

OKLAHOMA   ARKANSAS

TEXAS

Twisters are graded from 0 to 5
on a scale called the Fujita Scale.

An F0 damages chimneys.

An F1 snaps telephone poles.

An F2 rips off roofs.

An F3 flips over trains.

An F4 destroys even strong homes.

An F5 leaves few things standing.

In 1999, an F5 ripped through
Oklahoma City, Oklahoma.
It killed 45 people.

The worst twister

In 1925, one twister in Tornado Alley destroyed four towns in less than four hours. It killed 689 people.

People in Tornado Alley are
well prepared for twisters.
Most of them have
an underground shelter
outside their home.

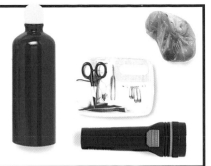

Some people in Texas have
a fiberglass shelter
buried in their backyard.

People without
a shelter hide
in a cellar
or small room
in the middle
of their house.

The Malone family
next to their
fiberglass shelter
before it is buried

Gary England is
a TV weather reporter
in Oklahoma City.
When lots of twisters
are expected,
Gary's team stays on the air
for 30 hours or more.

Scientists tell Gary
what the weather will be.
Gary can then tell viewers.
The scientists use a computer
to help them forecast twisters.
The computer makes a picture
that shows where a twister is
and how fast it is traveling.

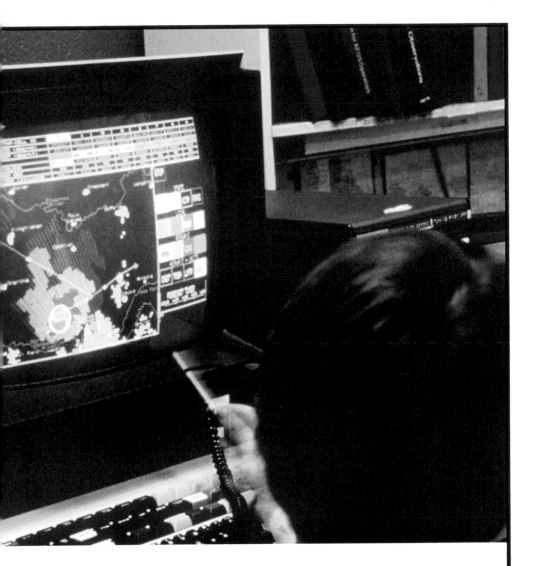

Forecasts from space

Spacecraft called satellites
orbit around Earth.
Some send information
about the weather
to scientists on Earth.

The scientists can tell Gary
what they think will happen.
But storm trackers on the road
know what is actually happening.
These people risk their lives
to find and follow twisters.
Many of them have
modern equipment
such as a satellite dish.

The trackers tell Gary
all about a twister –
where it is
and where it is going.
They can even tell him
when a twister is brewing.

In the past, people did not know when a twister was coming. Today, the trackers and scientists give people time to find shelter, and hundreds of lives are saved.

A storm tracker's modern truck

Twister facts

People in Tornado Alley
can check for twisters
when they fill their cars
with gasoline.
Many pumps show
the weather forecast
on a screen.

Winds inside a twister
can spin around
at up to 300 miles per hour.

In April 1974,
148 tornados tore through
13 states in the U.S.
Six of them were F5s –
the strongest type of tornado.

In 1994, in Australia,
hundreds of fish fell
from the sky.
This was probably
the work of a twister.

Twisters that suck up
sand in deserts
are called dust devils.

A twister can last
for any length of time –
from a few minutes
to an hour.